Spelling Seven

An Interactive Vocabulary & Spelling Workbook for 12-14 Year Olds.

(With AudioBook Lessons)

By

Bukky Ekine-Ogunlana

www.tcecpublishing.com

© Copyright Bukky Ekine-Ogunlana 2024 – All rights reserved.

The content of this book may not be reproduced, duplicated, or transmitted without direct written permission from the author or the publisher. Under no circumstance will any blame or legal responsibility be held against the publisher, or author, for any damages, reparation, or monetary loss due to the information contained within this book. Either directly or indirectly. You are responsible for your own choices, actions, and results.

ISBN 978-1-4466-1462-4

Legal Notice:

This book is copyright protected. This book is only for personal use. You cannot amend, distribute, sell, use, quote, or paraphrase any part, or the content within this book, without the consent of the author or publisher.

Disclaimer Notice:

Please note the information contained within this document is for educational and entertainment purposes only. All effort has been executed to present accurate, up-to-date, reliable, and complete information. No warranties of any kind are declared or implied. Readers acknowledge that the author is not engaging in the rendering of legal, financial, medical, or professional advice. The content within this book has been derived from various sources. Please consult a licensed professional before attempting any techniques outlined in this book.

By reading this document, the reader agrees that under no circumstances is the author responsible for any direct or indirect losses incurred as a result of the use of the information contained within this document, including, but not limited to, errors, omissions, or inaccuracies.

Published by
TCEC Publishing

Table of Contents

Dedication 7
Introduction 8

Spelling 7 - 1 9
Spelling 7 - 2 13
Spelling 7 - 3 17
Spelling 7 - 4 21
Spelling 7 - 5 25
Spelling 7 - 6 29
Spelling 7 - 7 33
Spelling 7 - 8 37
Spelling 7 - 9 41
Spelling 7 - 10 45
Spelling 7 - 11 49
Spelling 7 - 12 53
Spelling 7 - 13 57
Spelling 7 - 14 61
Spelling 7 - 15 65
Spelling 7 - 16 69
Spelling 7 - 17 73
Spelling 7 - 18 77
Spelling 7 - 19 81
Spelling 7 - 20 85

Table of Contents

Spelling 7 - 21 89

Spelling 7 - 22 93

Spelling 7 - 23 97

Spelling 7 - 24 101

Spelling 7 - 25 105

Spelling 7 - 26 109

Spelling 7 - 27 113

Spelling 7 - 28 117

Spelling 7 - 29 121

Spelling 7 - 30 125

Spelling 7 - 31 129

Spelling 7 - 32 133

Spelling 7 - 33 137

Spelling 7 - 34 141

Spelling 7 - 35 145

Spelling 7 - 36 149

Spelling 7 - 37 153

Spelling 7 - 38 157

Spelling 7 - 39 161

Spelling 7 - 40 165

Table of Contents

Spelling 7 - 41 169
Spelling 7 - 42 173
Spelling 7 - 43 177
Spelling 7 - 44 181
Spelling 7 - 45 185
Spelling 7 - 46 189
Spelling 7 - 47 193
Spelling 7 - 48 197
Spelling 7 - 49 201
Spelling 7 - 50 205
Spelling 7 - 51 209
Spelling 7 - 52 213
Spelling 7 - 53 217
Spelling 7 - 54 221
Spelling 7 - 55 225
Spelling 7 - 56 229

Conclusion 233
Answers..235
Other Books You'll Love! 263
Audiobooks 267
Facebook Community 268
References 270

Dedication

This book is dedicated to our three exceptional children and all the beautiful children worldwide who have passed through the T.C.E.C 6-16 years programme over the years. Thank you for the opportunity to serve you and invest in your colourful and bright future.

Introduction

Here you are, having made it to the seventh book of the Spelling for Kids series.

In Spelling seven, three hundred new words are waiting for you to conquer them. It is ideal for twelve-year-olds and teenagers. .....

You know the way. You know the motto.

Hear, Read, Write, Check. And repeat. Don't forget to repeat. Repetition is "a must" since, by now, you have added many new words to your vocabulary.

It would be best if you remember them. And the only way to do that is by making revisions. Bring a friend to study together and check with each other.

Turn the whole process into a game, and everything will come more easily to you.

Spelling 7-1

1. Spell:

Benedict was able to behave herself in her teacher's _____ .

2. Spell:

The opponents tried hard to _____ the team but they were united in their goal.

3. Spell:

Freya launched into a furious _____ because of how she had been treated.

Spelling 7-1

4. Spell:

Benedicta is a decent lady of

_____ gesture.

5. Spell:

Shooters escorted the _____

as he stepped out of the plane.

6. Spell:

All of the money was kept in the bank's

_____ .

Spelling 7-1

7. Spell:

The British Airways plane _____ down the runway.

8. Spell:

The homework was not _____, so Katie had to do it again.

9. Spell:

Davies was hungry, and he _____ all the food on his plate.

Spelling 7-1

10. Spell:

Thomas _____ all his information and data from various sources.

11. Spell:

Emily's father _____ the idea that she was old enough to set her curfews.

12. Spell:

You do not need to be a _____ to see that Chloe and John's plan will not work.

You've done it! You completed lesson 1.

Spelling 7-2

1. Spell:

The _____ stood to sing a hymn for the church's Sunday worship.

2. Spell:

The cashier checked that the signature on the cheque was an _____ one.

3. Spell:

Molly was angry with Jackson for trying to _____ her.

Spelling 7-2

4. Spell:
The government had to impose a twenty-four-hour _____ throughout the state.

5. Spell:
Harry was _____ about his opinion and refused to listen to no one else.

6. Spell:
Orchard was happy and delighted to _____ Cooper in his house.

Spelling 7-2

7. Spell:

Richard did not type in the

_____ PIN, so he

could not withdraw his money.

8. Spell:

Charles was able to _____

level eight in his swimming with

much practice.

9. Spell:

Caitlin watched the snake

_____ across the

garden.

Spelling 7-2

10. Spell:

The French _____ that killed a lot of people was bloody.

11. Spell:

Scott put out a lot of _____ on his first point in his argument.

12. Spell:

Mia _____ the data and was able to use it for her presentation.

Well done for completing lesson 2!

Spelling 7-3

1. Spell:

An _____ is someone who lacks basic literacy and numeracy skills.

2. Spell:

Allen saw _____ faces looking through the window to see what he would do.

3. Spell:

Joe _____ to be a teacher but has changed his mind.

Spelling 7-3

4. Spell:

Camron was humble enough to _____ his fault in making the wrong calculations.

5. Spell:

Dennis is an _____ boy.

6. Spell:

The _____ had ten fishes in it.

Spelling 7-3

7. Spell:

The south-End beach was _____ with teenagers on Saturday.

8. Spell:

Tim has been working hard on his _____, which is due tomorrow.

9. Spell:

Bobby is a _____ child.

Spelling 7-3

10. Spell:

Skye is a racist _____ ; she does not like to speak to anyone who is not her race.

11. Spell:

Isla broke the curfew and, _____ , did not have her phone for two weeks.

12. Spell:

Mr. Bradley made some_____ changes to his house, selling it at a higher price.

Well done for completing lesson 3!

Spelling 7-4

1. Spell:
The _____ predicted a mild rain the next day.

2. Spell:
Millie is considering changing her _____ from a teacher to a study coach.

3. Spell:
Callum was authorized to look into the _____ number of complaints he received.

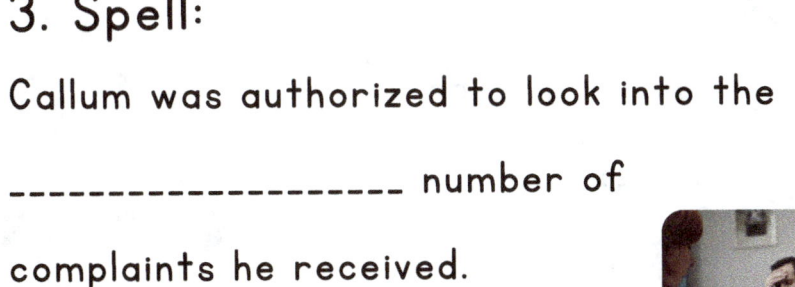

Spelling 7-4

4. Spell:
Sofia spent her _____ career in one school.

5. Spell:
Mobile phones have become an _____ part of human life.

6. Spell:
Archie tried hard to act _____ , but his eyes were full of mischief.

spelling 7-4

7. Spell:

An _____ view of Sydney

shows how beautiful it is.

8. Spell:

Riley has never flown on an

_____ before.

9. Spell:

George was quite _____

with the new plan.

Spelling 7-4

10. Spell:

Lennie could read and write wholly but decently _____.

11. Spell:

It was unkind of Abigail to _____ Luke's level 9 achievement.

12. Spell:

Billy saw the mouse trying to _____ under the door.

You've made it! You completed lesson 4.

Spelling 7-5

1. Spell:
Nathan tried hard not to _____ the truth when asked questions on politics.

2. Spell:
Lennie wrote a _____ letter to the school about her health.

3. Spell:
Ella did not have Tony's email _____ , so she could not contact him during the summer.

Spelling 7-5

4. Spell:

Lois went to _____ Betsy if she would come along with her for a stroll to the mall.

5. Spell:

Madison asked the lab _____ for help with her experiment.

6. Spell:

Jacob ceased to be a member of the _____.

Spelling 7-5

7. Spell:
Harris is the best _____ in his school.

8. Spell:
Connie ought not to have brought up the old _____ that she brought up.

9. Spell:
Harry has had sleep _____ which is resulting in his disorderliness.

spelling 7-5

10. Spell:
Alan drew a symbol to represent an Egyptian _____ in his artwork.

11. Spell:
Smith seems to have so much _____ towards Thomas.

12. Spell:
Alex offered his _____ to Logan for being re-elected as the team leader.

You have done excellent job finishing words in lesson 5.

Spelling 7-6

1. Spell:
Watch out! Turner is in a

_____ mood.

2. Spell:
Martin was wearing an army uniform

_____ .

3. Spell:
Mr. Hayes was awed by Owen's

_____ words to him.

Spelling 7-6

4. Spell:

Abigail, a gorgeous bride, walked down the _____ to the altar.

5. Spell:

Twenty-five laptops were the total _____ that was given to the new school.

6. Spell:

Amelia was _____ that the rain would not stop at a good time for her barbeque.

Spelling 7-6

7. Spell:
Oliver found it easy to _____ the new computer.

8. Spell:
The cable company offered Benjamin free _____ .

9. Spell:
It is _____ that Camron was harassed and murdered.

Spelling 7-6

10. Spell:

Harris was given the mandate to _____ two people in the class.

11. Spell:

Mr. Martins was _____ on meeting Charlene's mum after school.

12. Spell:

Riley managed to work on his school project for three hours without _____ .

Great work!

Spelling 7-7

1. Spell:
Sophie kept telling Chloe _____ facts that did not have to do with her.

2. Spell:
Alan ran into Davies, an old _____ in the shopping mall.

3. Spell:
Evelyn and John, who got married last week, are planning to _____ a new home.

Spelling 7-7

4. Spell:

Lois and Mille are walking_____ the street.

5. Spell:

Mr. and Mrs. Gibson will _____ their childminder to pick up their kids from school.

6. Spell:

Mrs. Gilbert will publish her new book in _____ next year.

Spelling 7-7

7. Spell:

George will be the next _____

of the town.

8. Spell:

Jacob saw smoke coming out of the

_____ .

9. Spell:

Harrison attended the seminar hosted by

the Institute of the _____ .

Spelling 7-7

10. Spell:

Hollie's doctor has referred her to a

_____.

11. Spell:

Mr. Pearson needed some _____

evidence before he could accept

Charlie's findings.

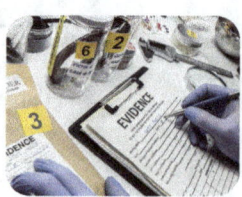

12. Spell:

Hollie was homesick, and that made her

_____.

Great work! You have completed lesson 7.

Spelling 7-8

1. Spell:
The _____ incident that happened to Smith has had a lot of effect on his mum's health.

2. Spell:
Thomas took Archie's phone and went to look at it _____ in his room.

3. Spell:
Alex is good at sports but does not like to play_____ sports.

Spelling 7-8

4. Spell:

All of Laine's stories do teach important

_____ lessons.

5. Spell:

The board members decided that closing the company would be a

_____ step.

6. Spell:

Connor's story did not have a

_____ of happy ending.

Spelling 7-8

7. Spell:
Sophie decided to _____ her friends carefully in her new school.

8. Spell:
Dina _____ Sophie as her new friend.

9. Spell:
Christina is the new _____ everyone is talking about.

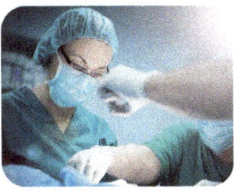

Spelling 7-8

10. Spell:

Cox _____ back in his comfortable chair.

11. Spell:

Leyton got a new job to work with _____ children.

12. Spell:

Mr. Adams is an _____ man who has taught Ted for five years.

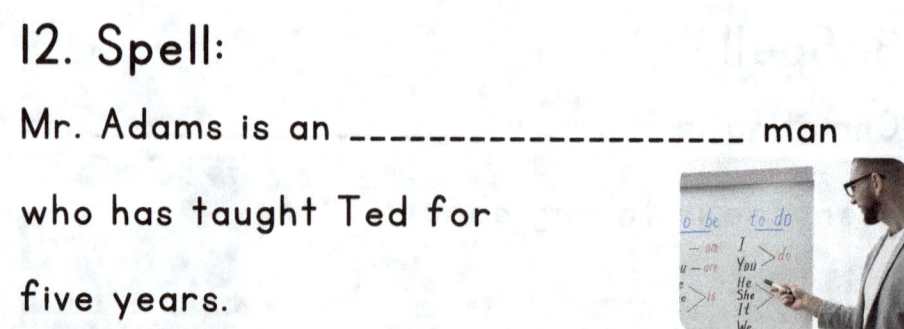

You have done excellent job finishing words in lesson 8.

Spelling 7-9

1. Spell:
Mr. Crooks was finally brought to book by the authority for his _____ .

2. Spell:
Colby's contribution was of great _____ to the overall performance.

3. Spell:
Luke's _____ was different from everyone in the group.

Spelling 7-9

4. Spell:

Mr. Grayling assumed an air of _____ to the topic.

5. Spell:

Chloe and Greg wore decent and _____ clothes to school on the non-uniform day.

6. Spell:

Noah added each _____ to get his final result.

Spelling 7-9

7. Spell:

Jacob's _____ look was on Scarlett.

8. Spell:

Mason believes in _____ because it gives freedom.

9. Spell:

The spot on Sienna's school uniform was very _____ .

Spelling 7-9

10. Spell:

Baby Oliver visited the _____

and was later admitted to the hospital.

11. Spell:

Chloe did not want to _____

to marrying Mr. Porter.

12. Spell:

Grace has scheduled an appointment to see

an _____ .

You have done excellent job finishing words in lesson 9.

Spelling 7-10

1. Spell:

Her vanity and _____ brought down Sienna.

2. Spell:

Alfie was sitting in an _____ position in the class.

3. Spell:

The weather is _____ today.

Spelling 7-10

4. Spell:

Mr Smith was in _____ when his son Alfie won the first schorlaship

5. Spell:

Addison tried hard not to look _____ .

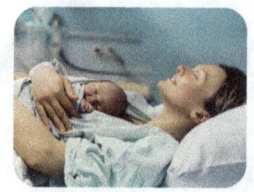

6. Spell:

Mai's _____ was not able to be present at her birth yesterday.

Spelling 7-10

7. Spell:

The school has its Sports Day on

_____ next week.

8. Spell:

Ruby-Lee was told to _____ and protect the plant for three weeks and report.

9. Spell:

The loud noise _____ Mr. Biggs.

Spelling 7-10

10. Spell:
John had thought that Riley was a _____, but he was not.

11. Spell:
Alan decided to wear a _____ sweater.

12. Spell:
I _____ in God.

Great work!

Spelling 7-11

1. Spell:

Khan is going to give her prescription to the

_____ down the road.

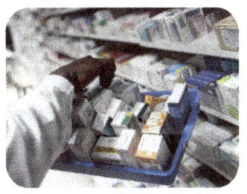

2. Spell:

Hard feelings _____ Elliot

and his father.

3. Spell:

Trey went to deposit the _____

he received in the bank.

Spelling 7-11

4. Spell:

Martin stood up to _____ cruelty to children in his speech.

5. Spell:

Skye found the whole scenario and situation so _____

6. Spell:

Colby is starting a new _____ selling shoes.

Spelling 7-11

7. Spell:
Aaron picked only one _____ out of many to have.

8. Spell:
Alice worked hard at university so she could break the _____ circle of poverty.

9. Spell:
The baby was crying hard, and the mother was _____ because she was in pain.

Spelling 7-11

10. Spell:

Dr. Marquis was _____ because he was always busy.

11. Spell:

Robison bought a _____ train ticket that could be swapped for next year.

12. Spell:

Emmanuelle was transparent, candid, and authentic in her _____ in all the transactions she did.

You have done excellent job finishing words in lesson 11.

Spelling 7-12

1. Spell:

Felix gave a _____ answer because he could not be bothered.

2. Spell:

Asher was the _____ person in the relationship.

3. Spell:

The _____ started in the canteen when Ava threw her bag at Ariana.

Spelling 7-12

4. Spell:

The mixture was not _____.

5. Spell:

Allison had to pay back the _____ debt to the government.

6. Spell:

The _____ was waving to the baby in his cot from the corner of the room.

Spelling 7-12

7. Spell:

Bailey and Blake are both

_____ , industrial, and

creative.

8. Spell:

Beatrice asked a _____

question and she got her answer.

9. Spell:

Bella is a brilliant and _____

girl.

Spelling 7–12

10. Spell:

Maths, English, and science are _____ subjects.

11. Spell:

The _____ music in the movie makes it evident that something terrible will happen.

12. Spell:

Brooke was _____ that Bella was watching her.

Congratulation! You have completed lesson 12.

Spelling 7-13

1. Spell:

Carter rode his _____ to buy snacks from the shop.

2. Spell:

Jamie has never met such an ardent _____ as Jacob.

3. Spell:

Hermione was _____ with her money by buying a strawberry milkshake for all of us.

Spelling 7-13

4. Spell:

Antonio is _____ coming home on Friday after his exams.

5. Spell:

Natalia busted out into _____.

6. Spell:

With light _____ on her feet, Georgia joined in to dance with the group.

Spelling 7-13

7. Spell:
Gilbert's _____ voice put off Teddy.

8. Spell:
Lyla dunked her chocolate _____ in her tea at breakfast time.

9. Spell:
The carpenter was asked to _____ a new cabinet.

Spelling 7-13

10. Spell:

Sara made the best life _____ by resolving to end the disagreement with Ella.

11. Spell:

Sara accepted the criticism with _____ .

12. Spell:

Drake and Dylan have changed their _____ on Facebook.

Good work!

Spelling 7-14

1. Spell:

Harry was able to _____ the incident that happened last night cleverly.

2. Spell:

Bailey will _____ to finish his spelling before playing games.

3. Spell:

Lily's room is _____ and colouful.

Spelling 7-14

4. Spell:

The _____ should invest more in creativity and talent.

5. Spell:

Ollie is facing some _____ challenges.

6. Spell:

Two of the _____ students are coming to the school in the summer.

Spelling 7-14

7. Spell:

The new role will _____

Oliver because that is not what he expects.

8. Spell:

Aiden is not getting any

_____ from his job.

9. Spell:

I am happy and _____ being

a singer.

Spelling 7-14

10. Spell:

Braydon was _____ about Elli- May's new idea for the summer holidays.

11. Spell:

Newman has a natural _____ to help his classmate through problems they face.

12. Spell:

Regan often faces _____ in the boot camp, so he has stopped going.

You have done excellent job finishing words in lesson 14.

Spelling 7-15

1. Spell:
Billy planned to _____ his friend, but he failed because he was smarter.

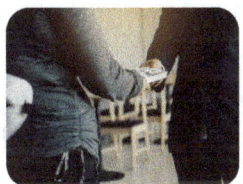

2. Spell:
There are a lot of_____ the body gets by drinking water.

3. Spell:
Camron had _____ from the state's scholarship.

Spelling 7-15

4. Spell:

Susan hid her face to avoid the

_____ that it would

show if seen.

5. Spell:

Katie was _____ to see her

brother return from his trip to

France.

6. Spell:

Ben's petrol _____ is on a

half tank.

Spelling 7-15

7. Spell:

Daisy left the room _____ after the conversation started as she was not comfortable.

8. Spell:

_____ ten is twenty.

9. Spell:

Bella will _____ seeing her result because she did not prepare well for the exam.

Spelling 7-15

10. Spell:
Julius is an _____ character who likes putting on dark shades.

11. Spell:
Samuel has been practicing spelling 5 to_____ his spelling skills.

12. Spell:
Logan and Shaw planned to _____ from the crowd through the back door.

Great work!

Spelling 7-16

1. Spell:

Alex was sorry to _____ his dad's expectations.

2. Spell:

Peter is a _____ of Jesus.

3. Spell:

Nancy heard the _____ sensation that she was not alone.

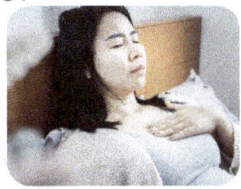

Spelling 7-16

4. Spell:

Rebecca is an _____ and dedicated swimmer.

5. Spell:

Anthony planned to _____ his friends when he walked in through the glass door.

6. Spell:

Mr. Lawrence is _____ rich.

Spelling 7-16

7. Spell:
Asher got _____ percent on his last test.

8. Spell:
Tracey did not _____ her part of the obligation that was initially agreed upon.

9. Spell:
_____, she failed her final exams.

Spelling 7-16

10. Spell:

Smith is always so _____ in the mornings.

11. Spell:

There will be the_____ , spelling, and punctuation test next Friday.

12. Spell:

_____ and hatred are emotions.

You have done excellent job finishing words in lesson 16.

Spelling 7-17

1. Spell:

Ansell has a deep sense of _____ for his former form tutor.

2. Spell:

Sophia took out her _____ from her bag and began to cry.

3. Spell:

Daisy could not go for the rides because she was afraid of _____ .

Spelling 7-17

4. Spell:

Nancie will be on _____ for three weeks.

5. Spell:

Maddie has a decent sense of_____ .

6. Spell:

The inscription of Sophie's dress was partly_____ .

Spelling 7-17

7. Spell:

Carter stood up and played an

_____ piano with

his hands.

8. Spell:

Max did _____ the figures.

9. Spell:

Carter drove carefully and did not

_____ the speed limit on the

highway.

spelling 7-17

10. Spell:

Everyone stayed back eagerly, _____ Leo.

11. Spell:

There are 28 days in _____ and 29 days in a leap year.

12. Spell:

Mason has a new job in a _____ store in the shopping mall.

You have done excellent job finishing words in lesson 16.

Spelling 7-18

1. Spell:

Nina's breath came in _____ gasps.

2. Spell:

The teen boys who planned the _____ ended up being arrested.

Davies and Darcie have been in relationship for the past four _____ years.

Spelling 7-18

4. Spell:

Their joy and happiness were to be sadly

_____ .

5. Spell:

Louie is a good _____

of character.

6. Spell:

Oliver has a _____ for

languages.

Spelling 7-18

7. Spell:

Daniel forgot to _____ on the door to Julia's room before he entered.

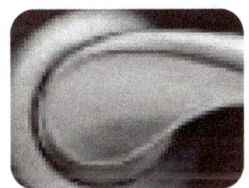

8. Spell:

The _____ center will be closed during the public holidays.

9. Spell:

Flynn has gone to the _____ to do research for her project.

Spelling 7-18

10. Spell:

Hughes is going to visit his

_____ at the

university on Saturday.

11. Spell:

Liam needs more _____ on

the subject as he is not

confident yet.

12. Spell:

The _____ party might win

the election.

Bravo! You have completed spelling 18.

Spelling 7-19

1. Spell:

There were _____ people at the national conference held in California.

2. Spell:

Dr. Patel had to _____ a series of tests to determine the cause of the problem.

3. Spell:

Macie is _____ at computers.

Spelling 7-19

4. Spell:

Alfie gave an _____ description of the project.

5. Spell:

William became _____ and withdrawn, hardly speaking to no one in the group.

6. Spell:

Julius has a _____ personality.

Spelling 7-19

7. Spell:
Jude showed some _____ traits when he was with his childminder.

8. Spell:
The pilot had to make a daring and quick _____ to avoid an incoming missile.

9. Spell:
I sympathize with Ronnie on his _____ .

Spelling 7-19

10. Spell:
Riley is suffering from a _____, stealing things because he has the impulse for them.

11. Spell:
Mr. Andrew was an _____, caught with stolen money from his client's account.

12. Spell:
Lainey requested the new _____.

You have done excellent job finishing words in lesson 19.

Spelling 7-20

1. Spell:
Smith could not _____ eye contact with the teacher during the science lesson.

2. Spell:
Courtney will be going to a _____ seminar at the weekend.

3. Spell:
The accountant gave Thomas some money to cover _____ expenses.

Spelling 7-20

4. Spell:

Tara would _____ visit Henry on his campus.

5. Spell:

It did _____ to Ben to write an apology letter to Elliot for shouting at him.

6. Spell:

The class was bubbling with much _____ on the last day of school.

Spelling 7-20

7. Spell:
Jayden requested a new _____ book for his work.

8. Spell:
How _____ of a fat trainer telling Hannah to lose weight.

9. Spell:
Aaron found the _____ he was searching for online.

Spelling 7-20

10. Spell:

Joanne is going to _____ with a fake cough in hopes of being excused from her duties.

11. Spell:

Laura interpreted his cold silence as _____

12. Spell:

Angelica enjoyed the _____ brought on by the talent show.

Great work! You have completed lesson 20.

Spelling 7-21

1. Spell:

Teddy's idea brought a _____ smile to Hilda's face.

2. Spell:

Joshua and Ephraim love _____ because of the teacher's styles and creativity.

3. Spell:

Jones spoke to Jake in a _____.

Spelling 7-21

4. Spell:

Samantha's _____ goal is to be a medical doctor.

5. Spell:

Victoria and Ellis have their _____ test tomorrow.

6. Spell:

Catherine is tired, miserable, and _____ .

Spelling 7-21

7. Spell:

Lauren finds it helpful and _____ to do daily exercise.

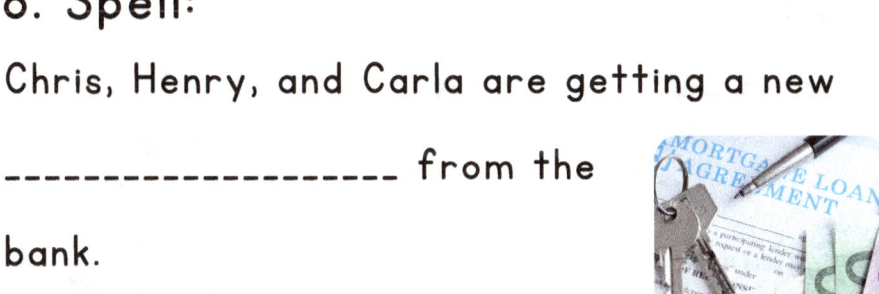

8. Spell:

Chris, Henry, and Carla are getting a new _____ from the bank.

9. Spell:

Wilson developed _____ difficulties, so he now wears a hearing aid.

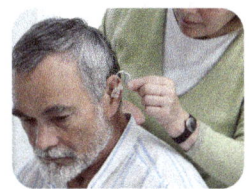

Spelling 7-21

10. Spell:

Scott does not have the _____ to be a good dancer.

11. Spell:

Graham got chatting with his new _____ for about two hours.

12. Spell:

Rhoda was left to _____ the new contract for the company.

You have done excellent job finishing words in lesson 21.

Spelling 7-22

1. Spell:

The spot on Erica's jeans was

_____ to everyone

present.

2. Spell:

The ancient _____ regime

was overthrown.

3. Spell:

Graham's attempt to expand his business

was a _____.

Spelling 7-22

4. Spell:

Terry's tone was respectful and

_____ .

5. Spell:

Mr. Richards, the head teacher, has brought

new laws into _____.

6. Spell:

Prescott was _____ busy

today with his football practice.

Spelling 7-22

7. Spell:
Cats do _____ baby Zoe

8. Spell:
It is not _____ to finish the work before the end of the lesson, so that we will continue later.

9. Spell:
A brilliant idea _____ to Lawrence while he was titrating in science.

Spelling 7-22

10. Spell:

Jokes are a rare _____ in Mr Evan's geography class.

11. Spell:

The _____ of Harriet's name from the register was not deliberate.

12. Spell:

Andrew was in _____ when he realized how late he was for his first lesson on Monday.

Congrats! You have completed lesson 22.

Spelling 7-23

1. Spell:
The basketball team will _____ new players in the summer.

2. Spell:
Cooper was sentenced to ten years imprisonment in the movie for _____.

3. Spell:
The past generation has suffered slavery and _____ attacks.

Spelling 7-23

4. Spell:
They attempted to _____ the president in the new film, but they failed.

5. Spell:
Andrew _____ and kicked him hard out of his room.

6. Spell:
The railway station is _____ to the shopping complex.

Spelling 7-23

7. Spell:
The famous actor was _____ through her role in her last film.

8. Spell:
Lilian was wearing a _____ outfit that her father frowned against.

9. Spell:
Liam did not _____ at the canteen staff.

Spelling 7-23

10. Spell:
Faye tried to _____ all the memories of her grandmother.

11. Spell:
The green snake _____ and hissed.

12. Spell:
The Headteacher has the _____ to admit new students after school starts.

You have done excellent job finishing words in lesson 23.

Spelling 7-24

1. Spell:
Playing Connect-4 is a popular _____ for the class.

2. Spell:
Clarke was driving at a _____ speed but still got a ticket that he was contesting.

3. Spell:
The actions taken were a _____ of their civil rights.

Spelling 7-24

4. Spell:
Lenny's walk was graceful and

_____ .

5. Spell:
Kelvin likes to _____ his

mum with his test results.

6. Spell:
Billy did try hard to _____

his yawn during the choir practice.

Spelling 7-24

7. Spell:
Alfred lay in bed all afternoon because of the _____ pain in his abdomen.

8. Spell:
The team has increased the _____ working on the project.

9. Spell:
Molly's _____ opinion on contributing to a class party was well accepted.

Spelling 7-24

10. Spell:

Rebecca was voted as the most _____ person in her form and year.

11. Spell:

William describes himself as _____ .

12. Spell:

The argument ended up _____ with all the parties involved.

Congrats! You have made such Progress! You finished the words in lesson 24.

Spelling 7-25

1. Spell:

Mrs. Marcus was _____ from the whole matter.

2. Spell:

Teddy _____ across the hall.

3. Spell:

Suddenly, a _____ shook Leo, and he fell to the ground.

Spelling 7-25

4. Spell:
Julius loves to watch _____ films.

5. Spell:
The school has decided to _____ all the products from the company.

6. Spell:
Mr. Harper's _____ of life is handwork.

Spelling 7-25

7. Spell:

Mr. Scott is not a _____, but he is a physics teacher.

8. Spell:

How many library books does Courtney _____ ?

9. Spell:

Johnson was _____ confident that his football team would reach the finals.

Spelling 7-25

10. Spell:

I wish Jay and Joy an _____ of happiness in their married life

11. Spell:

The young man struggled to defeat his _____ in the final round.

12. Spell:

Susan's foreign accent was barely _____ .

Congrats! You finished the words in lesson 25.

Spelling 7-26

1. Spell:

Stephan received an _____ welcome when he arrived in Cameroon for the first time.

2. Spell:

Jamie spent his afternoon counselling his _____ friend.

3. Spell:

Theo's class work was to design a _____ for his project.

Spelling 7-26

4. Spell:

Daniella has made up her mind to _____ a medical degree.

5. Spell:

The ship was tied to the _____ with a thick rope.

6. Spell:

Tony had _____ his lines, but the lines evaded him.

Spelling 7-26

7. Spell:
Kelly will _____ an email from his bank today.

8. Spell:
Daniel had to join the _____ to buy his ticket for the concert.

9. Spell:
What Lucas was suggesting is beyond the _____ of possibilities.

Spelling 7-26

10. Spell:

Ruby leaned back on the couch to

_____ Susan that

all would be well.

11. Spell:

Betty has a postgraduate degree in

_____ .

12. Spell:

Tegan was given her _____

after she paid for her meals.

Congrats! You have made such Progress! You finished the words in lesson 26.

Spelling 7-27

1. Spell:
Lily has _____ an appointment to see her doctor.

2. Spell:
Debby tried hard to _____ the ball from Jacob.

3. Spell:
Nathaniel was put in a _____ room to isolate him from others.

Spelling 7-27

4. Spell:

Do not be such a _____!

5. Spell:

Beatrice was one of the _____ of the last plane crash given to the new school.

6. Spell:

Earnest is given to _____.

Spelling 7-27

7. Spell:

Libby is suffering from chronic

_____ .

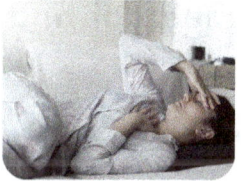

8. Spell:

Khan is showing _____

behavior.

9. Spell:

Jonathan's _____ makes it

difficult to bear up with him.

Spelling 7-27

10. Spell:

Ben has an _____ faith in the medical and health benefits of ginger.

11. Spell:

A _____ way to say 'you are fired' is 'We are letting you go.'

12. Spell:

Sonny filled in his name, age, and _____ on the application.

Congrats! You finished the words in lesson 27.

Spelling 7-28

1. Spell:

Dan is an _____ who thinks he is doing everything for the best.

2. Spell:

Harriet's problem is _____ to Henry's.

3. Spell:

He seems _____ with his intentions.

Spelling 7-28

4. Spell:

The boys loved their outfits, and their sense of joy was _____ .

5. Spell:

All the travel expenses were _____ from the company.

6. Spell:

If you shout and yell back, it will only _____ more arguments.

Spelling 7-28

7. Spell:

The whole country has been in

_____ for the

past few years.

8. Spell:

The homeless woman lived in

_____ because

she did not have running water.

9. Spell:

Nathan struggled to _____

his thoughts.

Spelling 7-28

10. Spell:

The nurse had acted _____ .

11. Spell:

Timmy was able to _____ ther teacher's contribution to her exam success.

12. Spell:

Sheila is hardworking and _____; she made up three fairy stories.

Congrats! You finished the words in lesson 28.

Spelling 7-29

1. Spell:

The gate man is such an _____ man.

2. Spell:

The damage to Jacklyn and Jack's relationship is _____ .

3. Spell:

The iron rod is _____ .

Spelling 7-29

4. Spell:

His _____ voice was used to show interest to the people around him.

5. Spell:

A _____ congregation sang the chorus at the burial.

6. Spell:

After Bernard delivered his _____, he was discouraged.

Spelling 7-29

7. Spell:

Libby has an _____ for science and further maths.

8. Spell:

The woman's performance was _____, making people book her backstage.

9. Spell:

She gave up a _____ surgeon career to look after her kids.

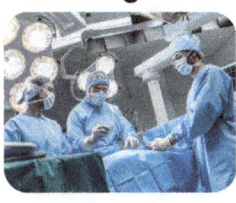

Spelling 7-29

10. Spell:

Jude attempted to _____

the canoe closer.

11. Spell:

Her_____ laughter stunned

the whole assembly.

12. Spell:

The greatest obstacle to her progress is

_____ .

Great work!

Spelling 7-30

1. Spell:
Jasmine had made all the _____ arrangements before she travelled.

2. Spell:
Grandma's _____ fingers spun the pink wool into a fine lovely thread.

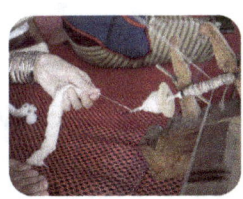

3. Spell:
The master of the ceremony tried _____ to keep to the scheduled timings.

Spelling 7-30

4. Spell:
It was _____ that Beckham would win in the finals.

5. Spell:
Elle packed out of the house because she was not _____ with living with her friend.

6. Spell:
The nurse _____ the afternoon drugs to all the patients in the ward.

Spelling 7-30

7. Spell:

His mum punished Leo, a teenager, because of his _____ attitude.

8. Spell:

Blake manages to _____ Jesse not to leave early.

9. Spell:

Jade had grown dull and _____.

Spelling 7-30

10. Spell:

John found the railways _____.

11. Spell:

The doctor will have to _____ some painkillers to help Joel.

12. Spell:

Luke had the _____ of meeting and shaking hands with the queen.

Bravo! You finished the words in lesson 30.

Spelling 7-31

1. Spell:

Do you have any type of questions before we _____ further?

2. Spell:

Julius is a teacher by _____.

3. Spell:

He appears too _____ for her linking.

Spelling 7-31

4. Spell:

Boris brought back a _____ from the rally.

5. Spell:

A vivid_____ spreads out before her.

6. Spell:

Joseph _____ smiled at Helen.

Spelling 7-31

7. Spell:
He was able to _____ his lost dog.

8. Spell:
The boy died of a _____ blow on his forehead.

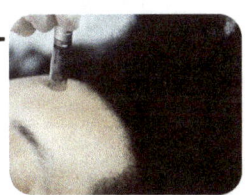

9. Spell:
Since its _____ , the nursery has educated over five hundred children.

Spelling 7-31

10. Spell:

Lydia was watching them play with cool

_____.

11. Spell:

Lead paint is an environmental

_____ that is

dangerous to kids.

12. Spell:

The children were looking up at the

_____ sky.

Congrats! You finished the words in lesson 31.

Spelling 7-32

1. Spell:
The film suddenly changed from being a _____ to being a tragedy.

2. Spell:
All students must _____ with the new laws.

3. Spell:
The winter tour will _____ in a spectacular concert in Greece.

Spelling 7-32

4. Spell:

They sailed into a quiet _____ bay.

5. Spell:

Jackson drove into a _____ car parked in front of the stadium.

6. Spell:

Janet went to the _____ shop to get some pens for the new academic year.

Spelling 7-32

7. Spell:

He intended to _____ the disease from his community completely.

8. Spell:

Hassan is a _____ dancer.

9. Spell:

Emily has no sense of_____ .

Spelling 7-32

10. Spell:

Abraham works hard so that he can

_____ .

11. Spell:

Skye had a _____ performance at the theatre.

12. Spell:

The music teacher's explanation was _____ to play the drums.

Well-done! You finished the words in lesson 32.

Spelling 7-33

1. Spell:

The features of the new phones _____ some of the personal laptops.

2. Spell:

There is _____ that Mr. Handy will teach science next academic year.

3. Spell:

Her _____ was published in 1981.

Spelling 7-33

4. Spell:

Mr. Martins resigned from the school, only to _____ three days later.

5. Spell:

Gracie has grown _____ about the challenges she has ahead of her.

6. Spell:

The stress of Stephen's final exams has made him a _____.

Spelling 7-33

7. Spell:

Sienna owns a private _____ .

8. Spell:

The three _____ will appear

in court tomorrow.

9. Spell:

Bryan gave his house a _____

cleaning last Saturday.

Spelling 7-33

10. Spell:

Stephan burnt his _____ on mushroom soup last Monday.

11. Spell:

Jake had to _____ the story to win Chris's compassion.

12. Spell:

Genevieve drew a dove as a _____ of peace.

You have done excellent job finishing words in lesson 33.

Spelling 7-34

1. Spell:

Christiana will like to investigate the Chinese

_____.

2. Spell:

Joyce will _____ Andrea for promotion after watching him for two years.

3. Spell:

Phil could feel his sense of

_____ .

Spelling 7-34

4. Spell:

Michael has a _____ nature.

5. Spell:

Clive does not need to result in _____ to win.

6. Spell:

Abigail's performance at the concert earned her shouts of _____ and applause.

Spelling 7-34

7. Spell:
Barbara was _____ to must have saved some money.

8. Spell:
Brian, the store assistant, gave a _____ smile.

9. Spell:
It is _____ that Camron was harassed and murdered.

Spelling 7-34

10. Spell:
Alan drew a symbol to represent an Egyptian _____ in his artwork.

11. Spell:
Andrea has a novel with an _____ plot.

12. Spell:
A _____ amount of damage was done to Mel's bicycle.

Congrats! You finished the words in lesson 34.

Spelling 7-35

1. Spell:

Chamberlain was given a general

_____ .

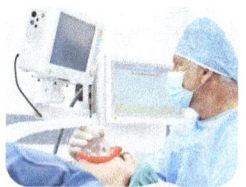

2. Spell:

The children's anthem has a lot of

_____ in it.

3. Spell:

He brought in an additional

_____ for the project.

Spelling 7-35

4. Spell:

Rowan drove to the _____ to have a decent meal.

5. Spell:

Matilda could not remember the _____ .

6. Spell:

Chantel likes the slow _____ of the songs.

Spelling 7-35

7. Spell:
The _____ situation is giving Camron a sleepless night.

8. Spell:
Daniel has booked an appointment with the company's _____ .

9. Spell:
The play's closing _____ takes place in the hall.

Spelling 7-35

10. Spell:

The _____ showed a forest.

11. Spell:

Amelia has got a new _____ job.

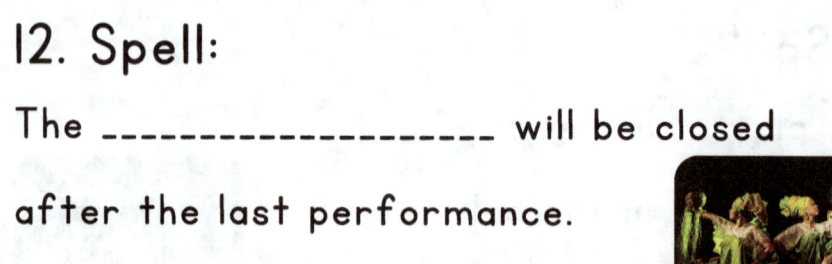

12. Spell:

The _____ will be closed after the last performance.

Congrats! You finished the words in lesson 35.

Spelling 7-36

1. Spell:

The police caught the _____ .

2. Spell:

Lewis _____ the story perfectly.

3. Spell:

Jude will be going to Paris _____ of London.

Spelling 7-36

4. Spell:

Benjamin _____ more time on his project than daydreaming.

5. Spell:

The Headteacher was able to _____ her intentions to the final-year students.

6. Spell:

The little girl was able to _____ her fears to her mother.

Spelling 7-36

7. Spell:
The history event was arranged in
_____ order.

8. Spell:
Ben used the _____ time to apologize to Ella.

9. Spell:
Her decision to quit school is _____ .

Spelling 7-36

10. Spell:

Any _____ you can give at this time will be much appreciated.

11. Spell:

There was a _____ danger from the start of the journey.

12. Spell:

He did not want to _____ to be the winner even when it was apparent.

Bravo!! You have made such Progress! You finished the words in lesson 36,

Spelling 7-37

1. Spell:

She invited her _____ class to the film.

2. Spell:

Lilly waited patiently as her friend _____ the given data.

3. Spell:

The king has made people obey his _____ laws In the play.

Spelling 7-37

4. Spell:

The _____ took control of the meeting for an hour.

5. Spell:

He rounded the playdough into a perfect _____ .

6. Spell:

They will _____ with their plans.

Spelling 7-37

7. Spell:
Lainey threw him a _____ glance.

8. Spell:
He went to _____ her cup with more fruit juice.

9. Spell:
Charles _____ his chairs.

Spelling 7-37

10. Spell:

Sienna was _____ sharply by her father.

11. Spell:

She has a very slight _____ on her chest.

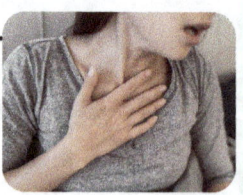

12. Spell:

Blake had to _____ the call because he was too happy to discuss it with her.

You have done excellent job finishing words in lesson 37.

Spelling 7-38

1. Spell:

He went for a _____

teenager's time out.

2. Spell:

Blake bought an extra _____

for his car.

3. Spell:

Isaac lost his _____ .

Spelling 7-38

4. Spell:

There was the _____ smell of sweaty feet in his room.

5. Spell:

Joshua was able to save all _____ expenses on his trip.

6. Spell:

Connor says a lot of _____ things these days.

Spelling 7-38

7. Spell:

They all will _____ at the hall for the seminar in the afternoon.

8. Spell:

The creature used a pair of _____ to locate its prey.

9. Spell:

Ryan was told to _____ from smoking.

Spelling 7-38

10. Spell:

The drink she served tasted

_____ and bland.

11. Spell:

Scott had to _____ the programme he was on before the computer could shut adequately.

12. Spell:

Caleb could _____ a knot the others could not.

Congrats! You finished the words in lesson 38.

Spelling 7-39

1. Spell:

Danny will _____ some money to the charity's project.

2. Spell:

Oliver _____ towards the door.

3. Spell:

The building developers destroyed the deer's _____ .

Spelling 7-39

4. Spell:

She smiled at her teachers with

_____ .

5. Spell:

She is a _____ young woman who has her way.

6. Spell:

She wore _____ clothes in the winter.

Spelling 7-39

7. Spell:
Sue was getting _____ about what her friends thought of her.

8. Spell:
David will _____ Abigail because she is diligent at her work.

9. Spell:
The family is _____ for paying their bills late.

Spelling 7-39

10. Spell:

Joseph's _____ is causing his parents loads of stress.

11. Spell:

He has shown a lot of_____ with his weekly spelling.

12. Spell:

At the teacher's _____, he left the class.

Congrats! You finished the words in lesson 39.

Spelling 7-40

1. Spell:

Dan likes _____ gifts, while Ella prefers spending time with friends on the phone.

2. Spell:

He felt a deep sense of shame and _____ .

3. Spell:

He was guilty of _____ .

Spelling 7-40

4. Spell:

She looked at the _____ from her window.

5. Spell:

She is proudly _____ to her class teacher for her support.

6. Spell:

When Alfie caught a fever, he became so _____ from it.

Spelling 7-40

7. Spell:

She was funny and _____ .

8. Spell:

Jude started his football career as an

_____ .

9. Spell:

Jacob's family is relatively

_____ .

Spelling 7-40

10. Spell:

He was _____ to the position of teaching assistant.

11. Spell:

Bella bought _____ to use for baking her homemade bread.

12. Spell:

Her _____ did hurt Jackson's feelings.

Well-done!! You finished the words in lesson 40.

Spelling 7-41

1. Spell:

The soil was rich, and It _____ rich crops.

2. Spell:

He spent about 15 years in each _____ sign.

3. Spell:

She slipped away from the house _____ .

Spelling 7-41

4. Spell:
Betty played outside _____ it was dark.

5. Spell:
She had a nice _____ of the car in her room.

6. Spell:
Barret has lost so much _____ because of her sickness.

Spelling 7-41

7. Spell:
Esther wrote a _____ of her stay in Paris.

8. Spell:
The new king decided to _____ his throne in the play and retire.

9. Spell:
The celebrity was ignored by Oliver as though he was a _____ .

Spelling 7-41

10. Spell:

They were exposed to a _____ accident.

11. Spell:

Daisy is an _____ , so she does not go to parties.

12. Spell:

The argument brought a lot of _____ among all the students.

Congrats! You finished the words in lesson 41.

Spelling 7-42

1. Spell:

The event was not recorded in her

_____, so she did

not attend.

2. Spell:

Tyler is now in a new _____

of change with his new habits.

3. Spell:

Sue has become such an expert with

writing _____

after several attempts.

Spelling 7-42

4. Spell:

Francis is a _____ book collector and reader.

5. Spell:

She _____ slipped the money into his pocket in the afternoon.

6. Spell:

A good smell did _____ from her room when she was dressing up.

Spelling 7-42

7. Spell:
Her handwriting was _____ .

8. Spell:
Ella has passionately _____ her dreams.

9. Spell:
Amie and Kyra owe _____ to their parents for all the help they give.

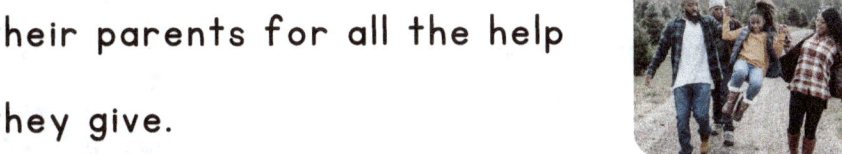

Spelling 7-42

10. Spell:

She gave us some _____ ,

which were a deviation from the topic.

11. Spell:

Rebecca has a deep _____

to return to her home country.

12. Spell:

Cecelia and her brother are more of an

_____ .

You have done excellent job finishing words in lesson 42.

Spelling 7-43

1. Spell:

A quarter of the city was destroyed because of a _____ fire.

2. Spell:

Thomas looked at the teacher, _____ .

3. Spell:

Dominic took a course to learn about laptop _____ .

Spelling 7-43

4. Spell:

Nina met an _____ young girl

5. Spell:

Dominic is a skilled _____ .

6. Spell:

The woman was suspected as an

_____ .

Spelling 7-43

7. Spell:
Mediation helped the divorcing couple to keep _____ to a minimum.

8. Spell:
David's _____ smile annoyed some of the people present.

9. Spell:
The drummer was also _____ with piano.

Spelling 7-43

10. Spell:

Two of the cats were _____ at noon.

11. Spell:

The _____ alleges that she was driving too carelessly.

12. Spell:

She listened to facts and not the _____ going around by the media.

Bravo! You finished the words in lesson 43.

Spelling 7-44

1. Spell:

The spread of the disease

_____ the doctors.

2. Spell:

They have received a _____

order to go back to their

country.

3. Spell:

Rita has been _____ in

choosing her friends.

Spelling 7-44

4. Spell:

Clara always has this _____ grin.

5. Spell:

Stanley has finally separated his business from his _____ .

6. Spell:

Jacob is taking the sick cat to the _____ in the afternoon.

Spelling 7-44

7. Spell:

The police are going to catch the

_____ .

8. Spell:

She moved in with her friend as a

_____ .

9. Spell:

We adore the family for their

_____ .

Spelling 7-44

10. Spell:
Nick hates the _____ of his job.

11. Spell:
Alice was _____ when she lost her husband at a young age.

12. Spell:
Ella is one of the most _____ girls in the school.

Congrats! You finished the words in lesson 44.

Spelling 7-45

1. Spell:

Noah was _____ in the finals of the competition.

2. Spell:

He was not able to _____ his children from the painful experience.

3. Spell:

They have formed an _____ within the neighborhood to plan events.

Spelling 7-45

4. Spell:

She is _____ for her dishonesty.

5. Spell:

Harvey comes from a _____ high-class family.

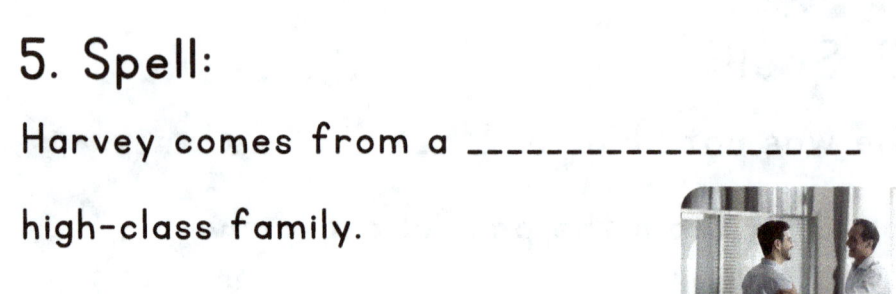

6. Spell:

The family is _____ and generous.

Spelling 7-45

7. Spell:

Phoebe made an _____

speech in the assembly today.

8. Spell:

Mrs. Harrison has made her work days

_____ because

of her kids.

9. Spell:

The agreement terms are both

_____ to the two

parties involved.

Spelling 7-45

10. Spell:

Stephan is strongly _____

against her.

11. Spell:

The old lady was advised not to do any

_____ exercise.

12. Spell:

The community summoned the

_____ to the

meeting.

You have done excellent job finishing words in lesson 45.

Spelling 7-46

1. Spell:

She interpreted the silence as

_____.

2. Spell:

The garden was designed with a new

_____ area.

3. Spell:

A new rule has come into

_____.

Spelling 7-46

4. Spell:

The class is going on a _____ school trip.

5. Spell:

Mr Palmers is a well-known _____ of music and art.

6. Spell:

A smile was able to transform his usually _____ face.

Spelling 7-46

7. Spell:
Finley pushed the botton, and the lift began it's slow _____ .

8. Spell:
The _____ will be played on Friday .

9. Spell:
The _____ will be played on Friday night.

Spelling 7-46

10. Spell:

Teens should have the _____ to make their decisions.

11. Spell:

Grandma suffers from _____ in her right arm.

12. Spell:

It was hard for Bradley to forgive such _____ behavior.

You have done excellent work finishing words in lesson 46

Spelling 7-47

1. Spell:

She has been able to _____

herself from this legal problem.

2. Spell:

She is influenced by _____

for her happy youth.

3. Spell:

The vaccine helped to provide

_____ against

yellow fever.

Spelling 7-47

4. Spell:

Sandra is an expert in teaching _____ .

5. Spell:

Martha is an _____ who takes business risks.

6. Spell:

Betty's gown was belted, which _____ the slimes of her waist.

Spelling 7-47

7. Spell:
The project requires some _____ planning with it.

8. Spell:
A cool _____ touched her when she was boiling.

9. Spell:
The _____ mother let Anne do whatever she wanted.

Spelling 7-47

10. Spell:

The prisoner was sick and

_____.

11. Spell:

Tina is a polite, decent, and

_____ young girl.

12. Spell:

Finley has been able to _____

a response from the public.

Good work! Keep it up.

Spelling 7-48

1. Spell:
The comedian welcomed his audience with a humorous _____ .

2. Spell:
Timothy's natural _____ has helped him to overcome the crisis.

3. Spell:
One of the _____ nurses in the care home escorted Alice to the hospital.

Spelling 7-48

4. Spell:

Daisy is an _____ feminist.

5. Spell:

Samuel and Libby are _____ for membership.

6. Spell:

Crawford's _____ makes it complicated to trust him.

Spelling 7-48

7. Spell:

Mason is older than them all, so he is more

_____ .

8. Spell:

Fin's company was declared

_____ because of

their inability to pay his debt.

9. Spell:

It is _____ that Camron

was harassed and murdered.

Spelling 7-48

10. Spell:

Isabella has a _____ hand for a grown-up adult.

11. Spell:

The organization has fallen into a state of _____ inefficiency.

12. Spell:

The ghastly accident was _____ .

You have done excellent job finishing words in lesson 48.

Spelling 7-49

1. Spell:

Owen answered all the questions in

_____ like "No" and "Yes."

☐ YES

☐ NO

2. Spell:

Frankie's time with Tia has left an

_____ imprint on

his mind.

3. Spell:

Their claim is being treated with some

_____ .

Spelling 7-49

4. Spell:

Lily and Rose went away after much hard work to _____

5. Spell:

Knowing our genetic _____ to diseases will not do any harm.

6. Spell:

Stephen was excessively _____ about what he had written.

Spelling 7-49

7. Spell:

The media have _____ the strategy used.

8. Spell:

Dan got compensation because the good was _____ .

9. Spell:

The traffic caused a _____ .

Spelling 7-49

10. Spell:

Every worker must log in at the reception under the new _____ .

11. Spell:

The girls were tired of being pushed around by _____ staff at the airport.

12. Spell:

Regular exercise has improved Megan's blood _____ .

Congrats! You finished the words in lesson 49.

Spelling 7-50

1. Spell:
The _____ game helps Aliya and Harvey learn about business.

2. Spell:
Alan's funds were _____ ,so he could not withdraw money from the bank.

3. Spell:
The noise was disturbing and _____ through the night.

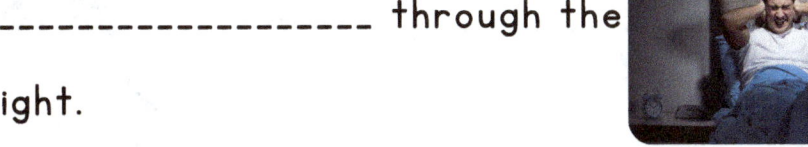

Spelling 7-50

4. Spell:

Evelyn has a _____ wound that is not that serious.

5. Spell:

Lois dinned in a Chinese _____ with her friends.

6. Spell:

Millie was focusing too much on _____ details in her essay.

Spelling 7-50

7. Spell:

The doctor was _____ that he would find a cure for the disease.

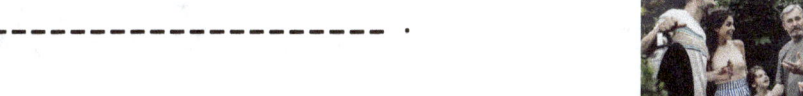

8. Spell:

The timing of the gathering was indeed _____ .

9. Spell:

The boys kept breaking the law without _____ .

Spelling 7-50

10. Spell:

Gilbert has a _____ for rich food.

11. Spell:

Fathers were told not to cause _____ amongst their children.

12. Spell:

Maddison is suffering from headaches, _____, and loss of appetite.

Well-done! You have completed lesson 50.

Spelling 7-51

1. Spell:

Mr. Martin was _____ from his country.

2. Spell:

Alice's job was to _____ the crime.

3. Spell:

A court _____ stripped Pearson from his military rank.

Spelling 7-51

4. Spell:

The children have an _____ desire to learn and know more.

5. Spell:

The war _____ enslaved people and preserved the union.

6. Spell:

Douglas went out of the hall for an _____ cigarette.

Spelling 7-51

7. Spell:

The hall has been divided by blue _____ screens.

8. Spell:

Grace did not _____ to the temptation of having chocolate cookies.

9. Spell:

Sheila was accused of making _____ remarks about Sally.

Spelling 7-51

10. Spell:
The teacher paused so that Dixon could find the _____ easy.

11. Spell:
There was a _____ of voices bubbling all around.

12. Spell:
The artist's _____ of the sunset was great.

You have done excellent job finishing words in lesson 51.

Spelling 7-52

1. Spell:

Alan was called a _____

because of his ambitious ideas.

2. Spell:

It is _____ that Yusuf will

not go.

3. Spell:

The negotiations have now reached an

_____ .

Spelling 7-52

4. Spell:
"Television" is often _____ for "T.V."

5. Spell:
Libby looked up the facts in the _____ .

6. Spell:
Sebastian and Kai have a _____ task ahead of them.

Spelling 7-52

7. Spell:

Josephine did not _____ to Joseph's marriage proposal.

8. Spell:

The police have finally caught the _____ .

9. Spell:

The _____ struck down the big tree.

Spelling 7-52

10. Spell:

The certificate was buried under

_____ papers.

11. Spell:

Oliver's screaming was causing a

_____ .

12. Spell:

Air travel has become an

_____ part of

the society.

Congrats! You finished the words in lesson 52.

Spelling 7-53

1. Spell:
Evans went ahead and _____ all the evidence to the head teacher.

2. Spell:
The road runs _____ to Asif Street.

3. Spell:
The missiles' blast was widely _____ .

Spelling 7-53

4. Spell:

Collins's speech was full of _____ but he  never made any direct accusations.

5. Spell:

Even though she told the truth, Rita did not find it _____ .

6. Spell:

Julie's behavior is _____ for an eight-year-old girl.

Spelling 7-53

7. Spell:
Chris's jokes were carefully planned, though they looked _____.

8. Spell:
Dan couldn't believe his cousins' house was filthy and _____.

9. Spell:
Jessica's mum was not _____ about the news.

Spelling 7-53

10. Spell:

Mr. Walker sent his _____ to his friend that lost his mum.

11. Spell:

Wilson _____ with his studies and got first class..

12. Spell:

Jay had a _____ about what will happen in his school the next day.

Great work! You finished the words in lesson 53.

Spelling 7-54

1. Spell:

Mr. William's staff finds him bossy and

_____.

2. Spell:

Mr. Dixon's decision has been made, and it

is _____ .

3. Spell:

Julius's writing is often _____

and challenging.

Spelling 7-54

4. Spell:

Stacy achieved _____ with the release of her song and instant fame.

5. Spell:

James is very _____ with his job, even when he is ill.

6. Spell:

They were all asked to _____ their identification card at the entrance.

Spelling 7-54

7. Spell:
The hall was decorated with stagy

_____ .

8. Spell:
The company was looking for

_____ Australians.

9. Spell:
Debra's uncle has become her legal

_____ .

Spelling 7-54

10. Spell:
Sally caught a _____ glimpse of the queen at the airport.

11. Spell:
Knight's narration was not _____.

12. Spell:
Jessica had a _____ view of firework display last night.

Congrats! You finished the words in lesson 54.

Spelling 7-55

1. Spell:

Sam is an _____ judge of their ability, making him a good leader.

2. Spell:

Lynn was _____ when she heard the test result that she had failed.

3. Spell:

Changing schools was a _____ decision Joshua had to make.

Spelling 7-55

4. Spell:
Laura was pleased with the elegant, newly decorated, and _____ hall.

5. Spell:
Ashleigh gave _____ to the cook for the delicious meal served.

6. Spell:
The doctor had a good _____ of the problem.

Spelling 7-55

7. Spell:
A _____ video camera recorded the field fight.

8. Spell:
The tutor was _____ and passionate about his work.

9. Spell:
The tourist visited the _____ garden near the museum.

Spelling 7-55

10. Spell:

Sue was adventurous by hiring a sailing

_____ .

11. Spell:

His dress was a perfect _____ to the shade of his eyes.

12. Spell:

Diane was _____ in the finals.

You have done excellent job finishing words in lesson 55.

Spelling 7-56

1. Spell:

Lisa reached to the _____ and spoke into it.

2. Spell:

Howard was always asking _____ questions.

3. Spell:

Harry's attempt at _____ the atmosphere was beneficial.

Spelling 7-56

4. Spell:

Sam accused Lisa of being

_____ .

5. Spell:

The _____ nerves help the body and brain to communicate movement.

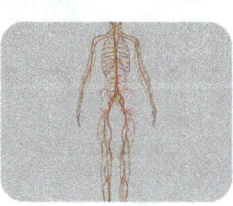

6. Spell:

Jenifer said a _____ good morning to her colleagues at work.

Spelling 7-56

7. Spell:

The crowd was impressed with the _____ Hughes used in his speech.

8. Spell:

The lack of adequate tools has been a _____ problem from the very start.

9. Spell:

Neon's _____ horror of flight prevented him from being with his colleagues.

Spelling 7-56

10. Spell:
Maisie's food was so burnt that it was _____.

11. Spell:
Leo entered the _____ as a young man.

12. Spell:
Jude is _____ to his boss.

Congrats! You finished the words in lesson 27.

Conclusion

Congratulations! You did it!

You completed Spelling 7, the last Spelling for Kids series book. Well done! Bravo! Hurray! You are officially a spelling Master because you put all that time and energy into studying and practicing.

By adding 300 more words to your toolbox with the help of this book, you should know about 2,600 words in total by now. What a number! Quite a huge one!

So, give yourself a round of applause. And ask for a treat. You surely deserve it! One last remark: Always remember that repetition is vital to make the words permanent.

So, revise the text to perfect your skills, especially the words that seemed most difficult to you. So, that's it, folks!

Grab your spelling gold medal; you are a champion!

Please leave a 1-click Review!

I would be incredibly thankful if you could take just 60 seconds to write a brief review on Amazon or the platform of purchase, even if it's just a few sentences!

Answers

Spelling 7-1

1. Spell: Absence
2. Spell: Demoralize (US) Demoralise (UK)
3. Spell: Tirade
4. Spell: Magnanimous
5. Spell: Fugitive
6. Spell: Vault
7. Spell: Accelerated
8. Spell: Acceptable
9. Spell: Devoured
10. Spell: Gleaned
11. Spell: Dissented
12. Spell: Genius

Spelling 7-2

1. Spell: Congregation
2. Spell: Authentic
3. Spell: Delude
4. Spell: Curfew
5. Spell: Adamant
6. Spell: Accommodate
7. Spell: Accurate
8. Spell: Achieve
9. Spell: Slither
10. Spell: Massacre
11. Spell: Emphasis
12. Spell: Analyzed (US) Analysed (UK)

Answers

Spelling 7-3

1. Spell: Illiterate
2. Spell: Inquisitive
3. Spell: Aspired
4. Spell: Acknowledge
5. Spell: Independent
6. Spell: Aquarium
7. Spell: Teeming
8. Spell: Assignment
9. Spell: Precocious
10. Spell: Bigot
11. Spell: Consequently
12. Spell: Cosmetic

Spelling 7-4

1. Spell: Meteorologist
2. Spell: Occupation
3. Spell: Considerable
4. Spell: Academic
5. Spell: Indispensable
6. Spell: Innocent
7. Spell: Aerial
8. Spell: Aeroplane
9. Spell: Agreeable
10. Spell: Innumerate
11. Spell: Denigrate
12. Spell: Scurry

Answers

Spelling 7-5

1. Spell: Evade
2. Spell: Confidential
3. Spell: Address
4. Spell: Ask
5. Spell: Assistant
6. Spell: Association
7. Spell: Athlete
8. Spell: Reminiscence
9. Spell: Deprivation
10. Spell: Deity
11. Spell: Animosity
12. Spell: Congratulations

Spelling 7-6

1. Spell: Belligerent
2. Spell: Camouflage
3. Spell: Solemn
4. Spell: Aisle
5. Spell: Amount
6. Spell: Anxious
7. Spell: Installl
8. Spell: Installation
9. Spell: Appalling
10. Spell: Appoint
11. Spell: Insistent
12. Spell: Interruption

Answers

Spelling 7-7

1. Spell: Irrelevant
2. Spell: Acquaintance
3. Spell: Acquire
4. Spell: Across
5. Spell: Authorize (US) Authorise (UK)
6. Spell: Autumn
7. Spell: Chief
8. Spell: Chimney
9. Spell: Neurologist
10. Spell: Dermatologist
11. Spell: Tangible
12. Spell: Docile

Spelling 7-8

1. Spell: Tragic
2. Spell: Discreetly
3. Spell: Competitive
4. Spell: Moral
5. Spell: Retrograde
6. Spell: Trite
7. Spell: Choose
8. Spell: Chose
9. Spell: Surgeon
10. Spell: Slouched
11. Spell: Delinquent
12. Spell: Admirable

Answers

Spelling 7-9

1. Spell: Treachery
2. Spell: Significance
3. Spell: Perspective
4. Spell: Indifference
5. Spell: Colorful (US) Colourful (UK)
6. Spell: Column
7. Spell: Predatory
8. Spell: Democracy
9. Spell: Noticeable
10. Spell: Pediatrician
11. Spell: Commit
12. Spell: Ophthalmologist

Spelling 7-10

1. Spell: Conceit
2. Spell: Awkward
3. Spell: Beautiful
4. Spell: Ecstasy
5. Spell: Vulnerable
6. Spell: Obstetrician
7. Spell: Wednesday
8. Spell: Nurture
9. Spell: Exasperated
10. Spell: Physician
11. Spell: Beige
12. Spell: Belief

Answers

Spelling 7-11

1. Spell: Pharmacist
2. Spell: Pervade
3. Spell: Cheque
4. Spell: Condemn
5. Spell: Hilarious
6. Spell: Business
7. Spell: Vegetable
8. Spell: Vicious
9. Spell: Helpless
10. Spell: Brusque
11. Spell: Changeable
12. Spell: Conscience

Spelling 7-12

1. Spell: Vague
2. Spell: Dominant
3. Spell: Chaos
4. Spell: Separable
5. Spell: Odious
6. Spell: Radiologist
7. Spell: Competent
8. Spell: Legitimate
9. Spell: Diligent
10. Spell: Compulsory
11. Spell: Ominous
12. Spell: Conscious

Answers

Spelling 7-13

1. Spell: Bicycle
2. Spell: Pacifist
3. Spell: Generous
4. Spell: Definitely
5. Spell: Laughter
6. Spell: Nimble
7. Spell: Strident
8. Spell: Biscuit
9. Spell: Build
10. Spell: Decision
11. Spell: Magnanimity
12. Spell: Profile

Spelling 7-14

1. Spell: Describe
2. Spell: Endeavor (US) Endeavour (UK)
3. Spell: Gorgeous
4. Spell: Government
5. Spell: Financial
6. Spell: Foreign
7. Spell: Dissatisfy
8. Spell: Fulfillment (US) Fulfilment (UK)
9. Spell Fulfilled
10. Spell: Ecstatic
11. Spell: Desire
12. Spell: Criticism

Answers

Spelling 7-15

1. Spell: Deceive
2. Spell: Benefits
3. Spell: Benefited
4. Spell: Despair
5. Spell: Desperate
6. Spell: Gauge
7. Spell: Immediately
8. Spell: Double
9. Spell: Dread
10. Spell: Eccentric
11. Spell: Develop
12. Spell: Disappear

Spelling 7-16

1. Spell: Disappoint
2. Spell: Disciple
3. Spell: Eerie
4. Spell: Efficient
5. Spell: Embarrass
6. Spell: Immensely
7. Spell: Forty
8. Spell: Fulfill (US) Fulfil (UK)
9. Spell: Incidentally
10. Spell: Irritable
11. Spell: Grammar
12. Spell: Grief

Answers

Spelling 7-17

1. Spell: Grievance
2. Spell: Handkerchief
3. Spell: Heights
4. Spell: Holiday
5. Spell: Humor (US) Humour (UK)
6. Spell: Illegible
7. Spell: Imaginary
8. Spell: Exaggerate
9. Spell: Exceed
10. Spell: Except
11. Spell: February
12. Spell: Jewelry

Spelling 7-18

1. Spell: Convulsive
2. Spell: Escapade
3. Spell: Turbulent
4. Spell: Transient
5. Spell: Judge
6. Spell: Knack
7. Spell: Knock
8. Spell: Leisure
9. Spell: Library
10. Spell: Niece
11. Spell: Knowledge
12. Spell: Labor (US) Labour (UK)

Answers

Spelling 7-19

1. Spell: <u>Ninety</u>
2. Spell: <u>Initiate</u>
3. Spell: <u>Adept</u>
4. Spell: <u>Animated</u>
5. Spell: <u>Pensive</u>
6. Spell: <u>Likable (US)</u> <u>Likeable (UK)</u>
7. Spell: <u>Lovable</u>
8. Spell: <u>Maneuver (US)</u> <u>Manoeuvre (UK)</u>
9. Spell: <u>Bereavement</u>
10. Spell: <u>Kleptomaniac</u>
11. Spell: <u>Embezzler</u>
12. Spell: <u>Catalog (US)</u> <u>Catalogue (UK)</u>

Spelling 7-20

1. Spell: <u>Maintain</u>
2. Spell: <u>Marriage</u>
3. Spell: <u>Miscellaneous</u>
4. Spell: <u>Occasionally</u>
5. Spell: <u>Occur</u>
6. Spell: <u>Excitement</u>
7. Spell: <u>Exercise</u>
8. Spell: <u>Incongruous</u>
9. Spell: <u>Celebrity</u>
10. Spell: <u>Malinger</u>
11. Spell: <u>Contempt</u>
12. Spell: <u>Nostalgia</u>

Answers

Spelling 7-21

1. Spell: Mischievous
2. Spell: Physics
3. Spell: Murmur
4. Spell: Ultimate
5. Spell: Oral
6. Spell: Lethargic
7. Spell: Necessary
8. Spell: Mortgage
9. Spell: Aural
10. Spell: Physique
11. Spell: Neighbor (US) Neighbour (UK)
12. Spell: Negotiate

Spelling 7-22

1. Spell: Noticeable
2. Spell: Totalitarian
3. Spell: Catastrophe
4. Spell: Cautious
5. Spell: Existence
6. Spell: Extremely
7. Spell: Fascinate
8. Spell: Feasible
9. Spell: Occurred
10. Spell: Occurrence
11. Spell: Omission
12. Spell: Panic

Answers

Spelling 7-23

1. Spell: Recruit
2. Spell: Manslaughter
3. Spell: Genocide
4. Spell: Assassinate
5. Spell: Panicked
6. Spell: Parallel
7. Spell: Immortalized (US) Immortalised (UK)
8. Spell: Provocative
9. Spell: Retaliate
10. Spell: Obliterate
11. Spell: Writhed
12. Spell: Prerogative

Spelling 7-24

1. Spell: Pastime
2. Spell: Permissible
3. Spell: Violation
4. Spell: Lithe
5. Spell: Surprise
6. Spell: Suppress
7. Spell: Excruciating
8. Spell: Personnel
9. Spell: Personal
10. Spell: Amiable
11. Spell: Agnostic
12. Spell: Amicably

Answers

Spelling 7-25

1. Spell: Exonerated
2. Spell: Tottered
3. Spell: Convulsion
4. Spell: Christian
5. Spell: Boycott
6. Spell: Philosophy
7. Spell: Physician
8. Spell: Possess
9. Spell: Supremely
10. Spell: Abundance
11. Spell: Adversary
12. Spell: Perceptible

Spelling 7-26

1. Spell: Enthusiastic
2. Spell: Psychiatrist
3. Spell: Questionnaire
4. Spell: Pursue
5. Spell: Quay
6. Spell: Rehearsed
7. Spell: Receive
8. Spell: Queue
9. Spell: Realm
10. Spell: Reassure
11. Spell: Psychology
12. Spell: Receipt

Answers

Spelling 7-27

1. Spell: Scheduled
2. Spell: Seize
3. Spell: Separate
4. Spell: Cynic
5. Spell: Survivors
6. Spell: Exaggeration
7. Spell: Anxiety
8. Spell: Cowardly
9. Spell: Arrogance
10. Spell: Invincible
11. Spell: Euphemistic
12. Spell: Occupation

Spelling 7-28

1. Spell: Altruist
2. Spell: Similar
3. Spell: Sincere
4. Spell: Heighten
5. Spell: Recoverable
6. Spell: Perpetuate
7. Spell: Turmoil
8. Spell: Squalor
9. Spell Articulate
10. Spell: Negligently
11. Spell: Appreciate
12. Spell: Imaginative

Answers

Spelling 7-29

1. Spell: Honorable (US) Honourable (UK)
2. Spell: Irreparable
3. Spell: Indestructible
4. Spell: Passive
5. Spell: Solemn
6. Spell: Soliloquy
7. Spell: Enthusiasm
8. Spell: Maudlin
9. Spell: Lucrative
10. Spell: Maneuver (US) Manoeuvre (UK)
11. Spell: Hysterical
12. Spell: Prejudice

Spelling 7-30

1. Spell: Preliminary
2. Spell: Skillful (US) Skilful (UK)
3. Spell: Desperately
4. Spell: Anticipated
5. Spell: Compatible
6. Spell: Administered
7. Spell: Disdainful
8. Spell: Cajole
9. Spell Staid
10. Spell: Deplorable
11. Spell: Prescribe
12. Spell: Privilege

Answers

Spelling 7-31

1. Spell: Proceed
2. Spell: Profession
3. Spell: Sophisticated
4. Spell: Souvenir
5. Spell: Panorama
6. Spell: Reassuringly
7. Spell: Identify
8. Spell: Lethal
9. Spell: Inception
10. Spell: Indifference
11. Spell: Hazard
12. Spell: Murky

Spelling 7-32

1. Spell: Farce
2. Spell: Comply
3. Spell: Culminate
4. Spell: Secluded
5. Spell: Stationary
6. Spell: Stationery
7. Spell: Eradicate
8. Spell: Professional
9. Spell: Style
10. Spell: Succeed
11. Spell: Successful
12. Spell: Sufficient

Answers

Spelling 7-33

1. Spell: Supersede
2. Spell: Speculation
3. Spell: Autobiography
4. Spell: Rescind
5. Spell: Complacent
6. Spell: Wreck
7. Spell: Yacht
8. Spell: Thieves
9. Spell: Thorough
10. Spell: Tongue
11. Spell: Exaggerate
12. Spell: Symbol

Spelling 7-34

1. Spell: Syntax
2. Spell: Recommend
3. Spell: Relief
4. Spell: Placid
5. Spell: Violence
6. Spell: Acclamations
7. Spell: Prudent
8. Spell: Supercilious
9. Spell: Arrogant
10. Spell: Incompetent
11. Spell: Intricate
12. Spell: Negligible

Answers

Spelling 7-35

1. Spell: Anesthetic
2. Spell: Repetition
3. Spell: Resource
4. Spell: Restaurant
5. Spell: Rhyme
6. Spell: Rhythm
7. Spell: Ridiculous
8. Spell: Secretary
9. Spell: Scene
10. Spell: Scenery
11. Spell: Temporary
12. Spell: Theatre

Spelling 7-36

1. Spell: Thief
2. Spell: Recounted
3. Spell: Instead
4. Spell: Bestows
5. Spell: Communicate
6. Spell: Verbalise
7. Spell: Chronological
8. Spell: Opportune
9. Spell: Regrettable
10. Spell: Assistance
11. Spell: Visible
12. Spell: Proclaim

Answers

Spelling 7-37

1. Spell: Whole
2. Spell: Manipulated
3. Spell: Unjust
4. Spell: Dictator
5. Spell: Sphere
6. Spell: Proceed
7. Spell: Contemptuous
8. Spell: Replenish
9. Spell: Renovated
10. Spell: Rebuked
11. Spell: Wheeze
12. Spell: Transfer

Spelling 7-38

1. Spell: Typical
2. Spell: Tire (US) Tyre (UK)
3. Spell: Umbrella
4. Spell: Unmistakable
5. Spell: Unnecessary
6. Spell: Weird
7. Spell: Convene
8. Spell: Antennae
9. Spell: Abstain
10. Spell: Insipid
11. Spell: Terminate
12. Spell: Unravel

Answers

Spelling 7-39

1. Spell: Contribute
2. Spell: Lumbered
3. Spell: Habitat
4. Spell: Gratitude
5. Spell: Wilful
6. Spell: Woolen (US) Wollen (UK)
7. Spell: Paranoid
8. Spell: Promote
9. Spell: Notorious
10. Spell: Behavior (US) Behaviour (UK)
11. Spell: Persistence
12. Spell: Insistence

Spelling 7-40

1. Spell: Tangible
2. Spell: Repugnant
3. Spell: Assault
4. Spell: Wreath
5. Spell: Indebted
6. Spell: Delirious
7. Spell: Indiscreet
8. Spell: Amateur
9. Spell: Affluent
10. Spell: Relegated
11. Spell: Yeast
12. Spell: Sarcasm

Answers

Spelling 7-41

1. Spell: <u>Yielded</u>
2. Spell: <u>Zodiac</u>
3. Spell: <u>Unnoticed</u>
4. Spell: <u>Until</u>
5. Spell: <u>View</u>
6. Spell: <u>Weight</u>
7. Spell: <u>Memoir</u>
8. Spell: <u>Abdicate</u>
9. Spell: <u>Non-entity</u>
10. Spell: <u>Calamitous</u>
11. Spell: <u>Introvert</u>
12. Spell: <u>Controversy</u>

Spelling 7-42

1. Spell: <u>Diary</u>
2. Spell: <u>Era</u>
3. Spell: <u>Dialogue</u>
4. Spell: <u>Voracious</u>
5. Spell: <u>Adroitly</u>
6. Spell: <u>Emanate</u>
7. Spell: <u>Illegible</u>
8. Spell: <u>Accomplished</u>
9. Spell: <u>Allegiance</u>
10. Spell: <u>Anecdotes</u>
11. Spell: <u>Yearning</u>
12. Spell: <u>Extrovert</u>

Answers

Spelling 7-43

1. Spell: Disastrous
2. Spell: Perplexed
3. Spell: Maintenance
4. Spell: Exquisite
5. Spell: Technician
6. Spell: Accomplice
7. Spell: Acrimony
8. Spell: Complacent
9. Spell: Proficient
10. Spell: Tardy
11. Spell: Prosecution
12. Spell: Propaganda

Spelling 7-44

1. Spell: Perplexed
2. Spell: Deportation
3. Spell: Indiscriminate
4. Spell: Inane
5. Spell: Colleague
6. Spell: Veterinarian
7. Spell: Culprit
8. Spell: Squatter
9. Spell: Generosity
10. Spell: Monotony
11. Spell: Despondent
12. Spell: Courteous

Answers

Spelling 7-45

1. Spell: Annihilated
2. Spell: Insulate
3. Spell: Alliance
4. Spell: Infamous
5. Spell: Respectable
6. Spell: Humane
7. Spell: Eloquent
8. Spell: Flexible
9. Spell: Advantageous
10. Spell: Biased
11. Spell: Strenuous
12. Spell: Debtor

Spelling 7-46

1. Spell: Contempt
2. Spell: Conservation
3. Spell: Existence
4. Spell: Geology
5. Spell: Connoisseur
6. Spell: Impassive
7. Spell: Ascent
8. Spell: Symphony
9. Spell: Claustrophobia
10. Spell: Autonomy
11. Spell: Rheumatism
12. Spell: Barbarous

Answers

Spelling 7-47

1. Spell: Extricate
2. Spell: Nostalgia
3. Spell: Immunity
4. Spell: Phonetics
5. Spell: Entrepreneur
6. Spell: Accentuated
7. Spell: Assiduous
8. Spell: Breeze
9. Spell: Indulgent
10. Spell: Emaciated
11. Spell: Respectful
12. Spell: Elicit

Spelling 7-48

1. Spell: Monologue
2. Spell: Resilience
3. Spell: Auxiliary
4. Spell: Ardent
5. Spell: Eligible
6. Spell: Hypocrisy
7. Spell: Culpable
8. Spell: Insolvent
9. Spell: Detrimental
10. Spell: Diminutive
11. Spell: Lamentable
12. Spell: Horrendous

Answers

Spelling 7-49

1. Spell: <u>Monosyllable</u>
2. Spell: <u>Indelible</u>
3. Spell: <u>Skepticism (US)</u>
   <u>Scepticism (UK)</u>
4. Spell: <u>Recuperate</u>
5. Spell: <u>Predisposition</u>
6. Spell: <u>Scrupulous</u>
7. Spell: <u>Exploited</u>
8. Spell: <u>Defective</u>
9. Spell: <u>Diversion</u>
10. Spell: <u>Regime</u>
11. Spell: <u>Officious</u>
12. Spell: <u>Circulation</u>

Spelling 7-50

1. Spell: <u>Monopoly</u>
2. Spell: <u>Deficient</u>
3. Spell: <u>Incessant</u>
4. Spell: <u>Superficial</u>
5. Spell: <u>Restaurant</u>
6. Spell: <u>Irrelevant</u>
7. Spell: <u>Pessimistic</u>
8. Spell: <u>Fortuitous</u>
9. Spell: <u>Impunity</u>
10. Spell: <u>Predilection</u>
11. Spell: <u>Dissension</u>
12. Spell: <u>Insomnia</u>

Answers

Spelling 7-51

1. Spell: Exiled
2. Spell: Investigate
3. Spell: Martial
4. Spell: Insatiable
5. Spell: Emancipated
6. Spell: Illicit
7. Spell: Movable
8. Spell: Succumb
9. Spell: Derogatory
10. Spell: Assimilation
11. Spell: Cacophony
12. Spell: Perception

Spelling 7-52

1. Spell: Megalomaniac
2. Spell: Conceivable
3. Spell: Impasse
4. Spell: Abbreviate
5. Spell: Encyclopedia (US) Encyclopaedia (UK)
6. Spell: Formidable
7. Spell: Assent
8. Spell: Culprit
9. Spell: Lightning
10. Spell: Miscellaneous
11. Spell: Nuisance
12. Spell: Indispensable

Answers

Spelling 7-53

1. Spell: Divulged
2. Spell: Parallel
3. Spell: Condemned
4. Spell: Innuendo
5. Spell: Palatable
6. Spell: Abnormal
7. Spell: Spontaneous
8. Spell: Sordid
9. Spell: Perturbed
10. Spell: Condolence
11. Spell: Persevered
12. Spell: Premonition

Spelling 7-54

1. Spell: Dogmatic
2. Spell: Irrevocable
3. Spell: Verbose
4. Spell: Notoriety
5. Spell: Tenacious
6. Spell: Surrender
7. Spell: Opulence
8. Spell: Indigenous
9. Spell: Guardian
10. Spell: Momentary
11. Spell: Coherent
12. Spell: Scintillating

Answers

Spelling 7-55

1. Spell: Astute
2. Spell: Demoralized (US) Demoralised (UK)
3. Spell: Momentous
4. Spell: Luxurious
5. Spell: Compliments
6. Spell: Analysis
7. Spell: Surveillance
8. Spell: Zealous
9. Spell: Luxuriant
10. Spell: Dinghy
11. Spell: Complement
12. Spell: Annihilated

Spelling 7-56

1. Spell: Microphone
2. Spell: Impertinent
3. Spell: Lightening
4. Spell: Vindictive
5. Spell: Cranial
6. Spell: Civil
7. Spell: Rhetoric
8. Spell: Perennial
9. Spell: Irrational
10. Spell: Inedible
11. Spell: Monastery
12. Spell: Servile

Other Books You'll Love!

1. **Spelling one: An Interactive Vocabulary & Spelling** Workbook for 5-Year-Olds. (With Audiobook Lessons)

2. **Spelling Two: An Interactive Vocabulary & Spelling** Workbook for 6-Year-Olds. (With Audiobook Lessons)

3. **Spelling Three: An Interactive Vocabulary & Spelling** Workbook for 7-Year-Olds. (With Audiobook Lessons)

4. **Spelling Four: An Interactive Vocabulary & Spelling** Workbook for 8-Year-Olds. (With Audiobook Lessons)

5. **Spelling Five: An Interactive Vocabulary & Spelling** Workbook for 9-Year-Olds. (With Audiobook Lessons)

6. **Spelling Six: An Interactive Vocabulary & Spelling** Workbook for 10 & 11 Years Old. (With Audiobook Lessons)

7. **Spelling Seven: An Interactive Vocabulary & Spelling** Workbook for 12-14 Years-Old. (With Audiobook Lessons)

Other Books You'll Love!

8. **Raising Boys in Today's Digital World:**
Proven Positive Parenting Tips for Raising Respectful, Successful, and Confident Boys

9. **Raising Girls in Today's Digital World:**
Proven Positive Parenting Tips for Raising Respectful, Successful, and Confident Girls

10. **Raising Kids in Today's Digital World:**
Proven Positive Parenting Tips for Raising Respectful, Successful, and Confident Kids

11. **The Child Development and Positive Parenting Master Class 2-in-1 Bundle:**
Proven Methods for Raising Well-Behaved and Intelligent Children, with Accelerated Learning Methods

12. **Parenting Teens in Today's Challenging World 2-in-1 Bundle:** Proven Methods for Improving Teenager's Behaviour with Positive Parenting and Family Communication

13. **Life Strategies for Teenagers:**
Positive Parenting, Tips and Understanding Teens for Better Communication and a Happy Family

14. **Parenting Teen Girls in Today's Challenging World:**
Proven Methods for Improving Teenager's Behaviour with Whole Brain Training

Other Books You'll Love!

15. Parenting Teen Boys in Today's Challenging World:
Proven Methods for Improving Teenager's Behaviour with Whole Brain Training

16. 101 Tips For Helping With Your Child's Learning:
Proven Strategies for Accelerated Learning and Raising Smart Children Using Positive Parenting Skills

17. 101 Tips for Child Development:
Proven Methods for Raising Children and Improving Kids Behavior with Whole Brain Training

18. Financial Tips to Help Kids:
Proven Methods for Teaching Kids Money Management and Financial Responsibility

19. Healthy Habits for Kids:
Positive Parenting Tips for Fun Kids Exercises, Healthy Snacks, and Improved Kids Nutrition

20. Mini Habits for Happy Kids:
Proven Parenting Tips for Positive Discipline and Improving Kids' Behavior

21. Good Habits for Healthy Kids 2-in-1 Combo Pack:
Proven Positive Parenting Tips for Improving Kid's Fitness and Children's Behavior

Other Books You'll Love!

22. Raising Teenagers to Choose Wisely:
Keeping your Teen Secure in a Big World

23. Tips for #CollegeLife:
Powerful College Advice for Excelling as a College Freshman

24. The Career Success Formula:
Proven Career Development Advice and Finding Rewarding Employment for Young Adults and College Graduates

25. The Motivated Young Adult's Guide to Career Success and Adulthood:
Proven Tips for Becoming a Mature Adult, Starting a Rewarding Career, and Finding Life Balance

26. Bedtime Stories for Kids:
Short Funny Stories and poems Collection for Children and Toddlers

27. Guide for Boarding School Life

28. The Fear of The Lord:
How God's Honour Guarantees Your Peace

Audiobooks

Are available at any of the following retailers:

1. Kobo
https://www.kobo.com/us/en/audiobook/spelling-seven

2. Google Store
https://play.google.com/store/audiobooks/details/Bukky_Ekine_Ogunlana_Spelling_Seven?id=AQAAAECiNH90zM

3. Libro
https://libro.fm/audiobooks/9798368981932

4. Audiobooks
https://www.audiobooks.co.uk/audiobook/spelling-seven-an-interactive-vocabulary-and-spelling-workbook-for-12-14-years-olds-with-audiobook-lessons/685234

5. Scribd/Everbrand
https://www.everand.com/audiobook/710833798/Spelling-Seven-An-Interactive-Vocabulary-and-Spelling-Workbook-for-12-14-Years-Olds-With-Audiobook-Lessons

6. Barnes and Noble
https://www.barnesandnoble.com/w/spelling-seven-bukky-ekine-ogunlana/1143432367

7. Spotify
https://open.spotify.com/show/62u0Jj6nv09gQBQ36ccMhE

8. Chirpbooks
https://www.chirpbooks.com/audiobooks/spelling-seven-by-bukky-ekine-ogunlana

And all other audiobook retailers!

Facebook Community

I invite you to our Facebook community group to visit this link and simply click the join group.

https://www.facebook.com/groups/397683731371863

This is a private group where parents, teachers, and carers can learn, share tips, ask questions, and discuss and get valuable content about raising and parenting modern children.

It is a very supportive and encouraging group where valuable content, free resources, and exciting discussion about parenting are shared. You can use this to benefit from social media.

You will learn a lot from schoolteachers, experts, counselors, and new and experienced parents, and stay updated with our latest releases.

See you there!

Your Free Gift

Your Free Gift!

As a way of saying thank you for Your purchase, I have included a gift that you can download at

TCEC publishing .com

References

[1] https://www.theseus.fi/bitstream/handle/10024/50239/Anttila_Marianna_Saikkonen_Pinja.pdf

[2] https://www.researchgate.net/publication/283721084_Early_Reading_Development

[3] https://www2.ed.gov/parents/academic/help/adolescence/adolescence.pdf

[4] http://centerforchildwelfare.org/kb/prprouthome/Helping%20Your%20Children%20Navigate%20Their%20Teenage%20Years.pdf

[5] https://www.childrensmn.org/images/family_resource_pdf/027121.pdf

[6] https://educationnorthwest.org/sites/default/files/developing-empathy-in-children--and-youth.pdf

[7] https://www.researchgate.net/publication/263227023_Family_Time_Activities_and_Adolescents'_Emotional_Well-being

[8] http://www.delmarlearning.com/companions/content/1418019224/AdditionalSupport/box11.1.pdf

[9] https://exeter.anglican.org/wp-content/uploads/2014/11/Listening-to-children-leaflet_NCB.pdf

[10] https://www.researchgate.net/publication/312600262_Creative_Thinking_among_Preschool_Children

www.ingramcontent.com/pod-product-compliance
Lightning Source LLC
Chambersburg PA
CBHW070649120526
44590CB00013BA/883